I0409925

PROSPECTS FOR DEMOCRACY AND PRESS FREEDOM IN HONG KONG

ROUNDTABLE

BEFORE THE

CONGRESSIONAL-EXECUTIVE COMMISSION ON CHINA

ONE HUNDRED THIRTEENTH CONGRESS

SECOND SESSION

APRIL 3, 2014

Printed for the use of the Congressional-Executive Commission on China

Available via the World Wide Web: http://www.cecc.gov

U.S. GOVERNMENT PRINTING OFFICE

87–704 PDF   WASHINGTON : 2014

For sale by the Superintendent of Documents, U.S. Government Printing Office
Internet: bookstore.gpo.gov   Phone: toll free (866) 512–1800; DC area (202) 512–1800
Fax: (202) 512–2104   Mail: Stop IDCC, Washington, DC 20402–0001

CONTENTS

APPENDIX

PREPARED STATEMENTS

PROSPECTS FOR DEMOCRACY AND PRESS FREEDOM IN HONG KONG

THURSDAY, APRIL 3, 2014

Congressional-Executive
Commission on China,
Washington, DC.

The roundtable was convened, pursuant to notice, at 12:09 p.m., in room 385 Russell Senate Office Building, Senator Sherrod Brown, Chairman, presiding.

Present: Representative Mark Meadows.

Also present: Lawrence Liu, Staff Director; Paul Protic, Deputy Staff Director; Andrea Worden, Senior Counsel; and David Petrick, Research Associate.

OPENING STATEMENT OF HON. SHERROD BROWN, A U.S. SENATOR FROM OHIO; CHAIRMAN, CONGRESSIONAL–EXECUTIVE COMMISSION ON CHINA

Chairman BROWN. Thank you all for joining us. Apologies for being late, and apologies, too, for turning this over after making a few remarks and hearing Ms. Chan and Mr. Lee give us some comments. Then I will turn it over to Lawrence Liu and Paul Protic will also help to run this roundtable, all on the record, of course. Of the two, I know Mr. Liu significantly better and the work he does especially. I'm so appreciative of how he has staffed this Commission and done such good work. So, thanks to all of you.

One of the great things about this Commission is that we bring in heroes who have shown great courage and have done very important work for freedom in their own countries and as role models for those around the world, and that's why it's my particular pleasure to meet and to introduce in a moment Ms. Chan and Mr. Lee.

I am reminded of that courage when we look at what's happened in the last couple of weekends in Taiwan, with students, at potential great cost to their futures and maybe to their safety, have done what they've done in Taiwan and Taipei. It's obviously very different. Hong Kong is very different, of course, in terms of its relationship with China.

But like in Taiwan, the Hong Kong Government is trying to decide and set a hugely important process and policy with little public input or little transparency. That's what they have in common, and it was the trade agreement with China and Taiwan. It's the process by which they will elect the chief executive and legislature in Hong Kong, and these are two people that represent the courage and heroism that we all are so proud of in this country, and around the world.

They are long-time public servants. They've devoted their careers for many years, pre-1997, since 1997, to Hong Kong's freedom and democracy. Again, I apologize, we're in the middle of a mark-up in the Finance Committee so I can't stay long, but I do want to hear their statements.

China promised to let the people of Hong Kong elect freely their leaders and enjoy the freedom of speech and freedom of press and freedom of religion. The People's Republic of China is backtracking on these promises they made to Hong Kong and these promises they made to the world.

In just three short years, the people of Hong Kong are to elect their leader, their Chief Executive, in the first election by universal suffrage, something that country after country, including ours, got to. I won't go into compromises of that universal suffrage that too many American politicians seem to be engaging in now, but we know that China is already placing conditions, sort of pre-conditions, on who can run, raising serious doubts about whether the election will be free and fair.

Mr. Lee, I know, had a very interesting statement comparing that to what might happen in this country if we had the same kind of rules. The environment for freedom of the press in Hong Kong is deteriorating. Incidents of violence and harassment against journalists have risen.

We have had a number of discussions in this Commission about harassment that sometimes borders into violence against journalists, how insidious that is. The Commission has made it a priority to monitor and report on developments in Hong Kong. We'll continue to do that.

We must hold, and this Congress, this Commission, must hold China accountable for its commitments and continue to listen to and learn from people like our distinguished panelists today. Too much is at stake in Hong Kong, and it's not just Hong Kong. You know what Hong Kong symbolizes to people around the world.

At the end of the day, Hong Kong is more than a financial center of 7 million people. It is a test of China's commitment to the internationally recognized rights of people everywhere to freely elect their leaders and to enjoy those basic freedoms that flow out of that. It is a test of whether China will allow genuine democracy and freedom to take root in Hong Kong.

We all on this Commission, and I can't always speak for Cochairman Smith, every member of this Commission, urged China to follow through on the commitments that it made in 1997 and the commitments that it says it has made since.

Let me introduce the two witnesses and then we'll call on Ms. Chan for five minutes, and then Mr. Lee for five minutes.

Anson Chan is one of the highest profile democracy advocates in Hong Kong. She served as Hong Kong's chief secretary, first under British rule and then after the handover to China in 1997. She was the first ethnic Chinese to hold that position, the second highest in Hong Kong, which oversees the civil service. She has been described as one of the most powerful women in Asia. She is currently involved in the Hong Kong 2020 campaign, which advocates for constitutional changes to achieve full universal suffrage.

Ms. Chan, thank you very much for joining us.

Ms. CHAN. Thank you.

Chairman BROWN. Martin Lee is one of the most high-profile advocates of democracy in Hong Kong. He is currently a top barrister. He is the founding chairman of the Democratic Party of Hong Kong. He served in Hong Kong's Legislative Council from 1985—prior to the handover—to 2008. He is also a former member of the drafting committee for Hong Kong's Basic Law. Mr. Lee, thank you. Ms. Chan, if you would talk to us first.

STATEMENT OF ANSON CHAN, FORMER CHIEF SECRETARY FOR ADMINISTRATION OF HONG KONG; FORMER MEMBER, LEGISLATIVE COUNCIL OF HONG KONG (2007–2008); AND CONVENER OF HONG KONG 2020

Ms. CHAN. Senator Brown, first of all, on behalf of Martin and myself, thank you very much for inviting us to this session. I have to say that both of us are very encouraged by your earlier remarks. This is the 17th year after the reversion of sovereignty to China and it is the 30th anniversary of the signing of the international treaty—the Sino-British Joint Declaration.

I wish I could say that everything is fine, but unfortunately, the reality on the ground is that ''one country, two systems'' is not working well. Two systems seem to be rapidly going out of the window. We have continuing and blatant interference from Beijing and from its representative office in Hong Kong, known as the Liaison Office.

We see our core values coming under increasing pressure and attack, core values such as openness, transparency, accountable government, a level playing field, regard for the rule of law, protection of the basic rights and freedoms that we enjoyed for many, many decades under British rule and which are protected under our constitution, the Basic Law.

In particular, we are very concerned at certain basic human rights being curtailed and coming under increasing stress, particularly freedom of expression, freedom of assembly, and freedom of the press and free flow of information.

So this entire quest for a democratic system of government is all about whether we can continue to keep a separate identity. That identity is guaranteed by the Basic Law and that identity has everything to do with the central pillars of Hong Kong's success as an international city and an important regional and financial services center. These are our core values, our regard for rule of law, our respect for human dignity, and for a whole range of rights and freedoms that you associate with a fully fledged democracy.

Hong Kong people value these rights. We have demonstrated time and again that we will not stand idly by if we see these rights being trampled upon. We have a whole young generation of people born after 1997 who have known nothing except life under Chinese sovereignty. They are politically savvy, they are courageous, they are prepared to stand up and be counted. Therein, perhaps, lies our best hope for a truly democratic system of government.

We know that the fight is very much up to us, but we think it is extremely helpful for our friends—in particular our friends in America—because we share core values with you and you have a stake in Hong Kong, you have nationals living there, you have huge investments in Hong Kong—we think it helps for you to let it be known to Beijing that you are watching. As you say, you are watching to see what happens in Hong Kong.

Is China going to honor its promises to the people of Hong Kong? It's a very simple request we are making and it is entirely doable.

Thank you very much.

Chairman BROWN. Thank, you, Ms. Chan.

Mr. Lee?

STATEMENT OF MARTIN LEE, BARRISTER, FOUNDING CHAIRMAN, DEMOCRATIC PARTY OF HONG KONG; FORMER MEMBER, DRAFTING COMMITTEE FOR THE BASIC LAW; AND FORMER MEMBER, LEGISLATIVE COUNCIL OF HONG KONG (1985–2008)

Mr. LEE. ''One country, two systems.'' One country was implemented at midnight on June 30, 1997, when the British flag came down and the Chinese flag went up. That is one country. But two systems have yet to be successfully implemented because without democracy, without allowing Hong Kong people to elect by democratic means their leader, the Chief Executive, and all members of the legislature, there is no way for Hong Kong people to rule Hong Kong with a high degree of autonomy.

Hong Kong people cannot be masters of their own house without being given the vote. Hence this urgency which caused us to come to Washington, DC. This, as I see it, is the last-ditch effort. Very soon the Hong Kong Government will decide—rather, the Chinese Government will decide for it—in what way our next Chief Executive is to be elected in the year 2017.

The Chinese Government no doubt wishes to give Hong Kong people the vote: one person, one vote. But they want to be assured that whoever wins must be Beijing's blue-eyed boy or blue-eyed girl. In other words, this person must fully obey Beijing's orders. How do they do that? They want to control the nomination process. They want to make sure that, through the nomination committee which Beijing will control, only two or three puppets pre-selected by Beijing will be able to run. That is what they want to happen.

That is why we have come to tell the people here—and we will be traveling to other countries too—that this is what they are trying to do, in breach of China's international agreement made with the British Government in the Sino-British Joint Declaration.

Now, we are not bringing a message of despair, although we have many serious concerns about what is happening in Hong Kong. We are bringing a message of hope, because there is still hope yet, if we can finally get it right, so that Hong Kong people will have the power to decide who is going to run Hong Kong in the future.

Therein lies hope, hope that all of our freedoms will be protected under the rule of law, which makes Hong Kong different from any other Chinese city, and also hope that China will implement international agreements. This will give assurance to the rest of the world that Chinese treaties count.

Now, to turn this message of hope into reality, of course, we, the people of Hong Kong, will do our part. We will do whatever is necessary to make sure that we, the people of Hong Kong, do become masters of our own house.

But the international concern which was expressed here, Senator, helps us to fight for what is rightfully ours and what is already promised to us by the central government. We want it to work, so that my vision for China can be accomplished, which is that the 1.3 billion people of China will have their freedoms acknowledged and protected by the rule of law. That is my vision for China.

Chairman BROWN. Thank you so much, Mr. Lee.

Ms. Chan exhorted us to "let it be known to Beijing, all of this." That is the charge of this Commission. We will certainly do that. I know that all of you watching—I hope those of you watching, listening, or those of you who are actually here, will do the same. So I apologize again and we'll turn it over to Mr. Liu to continue the roundtable.

Ms. CHAN. Thank you so much, Senator.

Chairman BROWN. Thank you so much. Ms. Chan, Mr. Lee, thank you very much. And Paul, thank you, too. Thanks.

Mr. LIU. Ms. Chan and Mr. Lee, thank you so much for your very important remarks. We may have other Members of Congress joining us. It's a busy day, as you know, with mark-ups and things like that, but in the event that other Members of Congress come, we'll give them an opportunity to speak as well.

But our roundtables are generally staff-led and we have some questions that we've prepared for you and hope that we can have a nice, free-flowing discussion. I have some questions. My colleague Paul Protic also has some questions, and David Petrick over here is on our staff and he actually covers the Hong Kong issue. We have a staff member who is in charge of following developments in Hong Kong, which indicates how important this issue is to the Commission.

Mr. LEE. And let us thank you for your help, for without your help, this cannot happen.

Mr. LIU. Let me just start with a question. We've heard about the Occupy Central movement, which may not be as understood here in the United States, just given how maybe not enough attention is being paid to Hong Kong. But can you tell us more about the Occupy movement and who's behind it, how popular it is, and what they're looking for? How do you think the authorities might respond if it moves forward?

Mr. LEE. Occupy Central is not the same as Occupy Wall Street. It was the brainchild of a young associate professor of law at Hong Kong University who used to be a summer student in my chambers. He got fed up with waiting for democracy, and one day when he was at a public seminar, which I also attended, he suddenly came up with this idea of Occupy Central. He said, "Look, we have been demonstrating in Hong Kong for democracy for so long, and Beijing does not listen. We've been holding hunger strikes, and they do not listen. We always like to do things peacefully. What must we do next?"

He came up with this idea of Occupy Central. He said, it appears that Beijing still won't give us genuine democracy, meaning democracy in accordance with international standards and also in keeping with our constitution, the Basic Law, which not only guarantees that the permanent residents of Hong Kong will be given the vote, but also the right to stand for elections, which are two sides of the coin; and you can't have one without the other.

So he says, "If we are not going to have genuine democracy after so many years of waiting, then let's Occupy Central." His idea was that large numbers of people will occupy the central part of Hong Kong so that traffic will be blocked.

And we'll be waiting for the police to arrest us. And if they arrest us and prosecute us, we will not fight the case. We will go to prison. I use the word "we," for I'll be there. So that's the idea. It has gathered great momentum in Hong Kong because a lot of Hong Kong people too, have been waiting and waiting and don't know what to do. What better thing to do than Occupy Central?

A lot of people say that it's like throwing eggs at the wall. And we are the eggs. We are prepared to sacrifice our freedom, which we cherish, and go to prison, so that we, and our next generation, will have democracy in Hong Kong. We are prepared to pay a dear price for it.

But the idea of this associate professor, Benjamin Tai, is that, hopefully, we don't need to Occupy Central, for hopefully, Beijing will see that it is only right for it to honor its promises already given to the people of Hong Kong and to the international community. So if it gives to Hong Kong a system of election which accords with international standards—and it will be judged by international law experts studying the proposal—then there will be no Occupy Central. So that's the idea: we will Occupy Central if there's no good proposal which satisfies international standards. If there is, then we will not Occupy Central.

Ms. CHAN. Let me just add one or two other remarks. As Martin says, it was a proposal borne out of sheer frustration and desperation. But ever since this proposal was given, there's no doubt that it has touched a raw nerve in Beijing, maybe because they are very concerned about their international image. The very thought that an Occupy Central picture will be splashed all over the international media, they do not particularly like.

So what they have done since then is to roll out the big guns and use every single means to demonize the entire initiative and the architects behind this proposal. Well, I concur, as on many other occasions, this sort of proposal, this sort of behavior only makes people sit up and take more notice. They've been exaggerating the economic loss and have warned of sheer havoc, as Martin says.

The government can easily avert Occupy Central. All it needs to do is do what it's supposed to being doing, which is, put forward a credible set of universal suffrage proposals, forge a community consensus, and secure the necessary majority in the legislature to get it passed. You then persuade Beijing that this set of proposals is the minimum that is acceptable to the people of Hong Kong.

Mr. LEE. And the organizers, of course, stress that the entire movement will be based on two things: peace and love. For they are Christians, who treasure peace and love.

Mr. LIU. Okay. Thank you.

I have another question. Hong Kong has now been part of China almost 17 years, and I'm just curious to know, since we have you and you have the pulse in many ways of the community there, how connected do the people of Hong Kong feel to mainland China and how is that playing into the current debates and discussions over universal suffrage?

Ms. CHAN. Well, economically I think there is ever-closer co-operation and some people who describe it as integration. Let us not forget that it was Hong Kong money and Hong Kong managerial know-how that kick-started the entire mainland economy and the power of the Pearl River Delta region. It may come as a surprise to some that even today, after four decades of open-door policy and phenomenal economic goals, Hong Kong remains the largest single external investor in the mainland.

People to people? Again, getting closer. We have millions of mainland visitors. We have an agreement with the mainland authorities whereby people come in on a one-way permit for permanent residence under an arrangement that has existed for quite a number of years, whereby we take in 150 people every day from the mainland for permanent residence. These are largely for family reunion purposes because you have people marrying mainlanders, so they want to bring their wives and husbands and they want to bring their children.

But in the wake of huge influxes of mainland visitors, and given that Hong Kong is only 1,000 square kilometers, of which about 40 percent is country park, and given the fact that our social and health services all have limited capacity, this huge influx has unfortunately led to hostilities. It is little wonder because we have mainlanders coming in, they sweep up everything in sight: milk powder, even toilet paper. Why? Because they cannot trust milk powder in the mainland.

So parents in Hong Kong who want to go and buy milk powder find that they have to go to several pharmacies and still cannot get enough milk powder. At one time, all of the maternity beds in hospitals were taken up by pregnant mainlanders so that Hong Kong women who wanted to deliver a baby could not find a bed at a suitable cost.

So this hostility is something that I think we in Hong Kong, particularly the government and also the mainland authorities, need to look at and work out because it should not be this way. If you take measures, you can reduce the degree of hostility because it is not in our interests and it is not in the interests of the mainland to have this hostility continue.

Now, it is a fact, of course, that with the growing economic clout of mainland China, the fact that the rest of the world all wants to do business with them, maybe they no longer feel, as at the time of the handover, that they still need Hong Kong. But there are others—there is a more moderate voice in mainland China which tends to be forgotten. Not everybody within the Party hierarchy speaks with one voice.

The leadership hierarchy is not monolithic. There is a more moderate voice. I feel that in Hong Kong, by sticking to our principles, to our values, we give encouragement to the small, moderate voice so that over time you will see improvements in human rights; you will see a degree of political liberalization, maybe not at the pace at which we want to see it, but nevertheless it will come.

So it is very important, important not just for us in Hong Kong, but important for China and for the rest of the world that Beijing is made to deliver on its promises that we have genuine democracy, because that's the only way of holding our Chief Executive accountable, that we can maintain a level playing field, the rule of law, and protect all our rights and freedoms.

Mr. LEE. I would just like to add one thing. I'd rather have them, the people of China, coming to Hong Kong to buy milk powder than we, the people of Hong Kong going to mainland China and buy our milk powder there.

Mr. LIU. I just wanted to introduce Congressman Meadows, one of our Commissioners, who is just joining us. I know he's very glad to see you guys.

Representative MEADOWS. My apologizes for being late. Thank you so much. I think probably for me, as we've started to look at this, is the challenges that we've seen from freedom of the press, from some of this stifling there, tell me how we can better encourage and use, I guess, our encouragement through negotiations to address those areas where we continue to hear a number of reports about not only firewalls, perhaps the need for those to not be put up or where we can breach those, the freedom of the press, some of the things that have been stifled. As we start to look at freedom overall, one of the key areas that I see is that whether it is with Hong Kong or with mainland China, is how do we encourage that freedom overall? So anybody that could comment on that would be great.

Mr. LEE. Well, freedom of the press, to me, is the freedom of all freedoms, because without it, no other freedom is safe. Nobody will hear about any infringement of freedoms if there's no freedom of the press. Nobody will hear what the government does to its people. So freedom of the press is the most important freedom.

Of course, we should not have to fight for freedom of the press in Hong Kong because we already had it under British rule. And the Chinese Government clearly promised the whole world that all of our freedoms will remain intact for 50 years unchanged.

But if we, in Hong Kong, cannot preserve our freedom of the press, how can we hope that the freedom of the press will ever be spread to mainland China? Unfortunately, freedom of the press has always been under pressure from Beijing. That is, I suppose, to be expected of the Communist government. One knows that all Communist governments simply do not like freedom of the press. They don't like people to know what they are doing to their own people.

And self-censorship has long been a big problem in Hong Kong because the Chinese Government has so much money. And recently the only truly independent newspaper in Hong Kong, called the Apple Daily, had its advertisements removed by international banks, because Beijing's representatives in Hong Kong, called the Central Government Liaison Office have been speaking to these banks and asking them to lift their advertisements already placed with the Apple Daily.

And some of those banks actually did what they were asked to do. And one such bank was the HSBC, Hong Kong and Shanghai Banking Corporation. Now, if even these international banks listen to the Communist Chinese Government and withdraw their advertisements from the only independent newspaper in Hong Kong, the erosion of the freedom of the press can only get worse and worse.

But it shouldn't happen like this. And Beijing promised that it would not happen. Unfortunately, we have to come here and remind the rest of the world that this is happening. Of course, we in Hong Kong will do our best to prevent this from getting worse. But we cannot do it alone in Hong Kong. We need the attention and support of the rest of the world.

Ms. CHAN. The fact that the Liaison Office is muscling in on the press means that there will be many who will toe the line because they feel that, at the end of the day, their business interests are affected.

There are very few owners and proprietors of media who have such deep pockets that they can afford not to toe the Beijing line, and these are getting fewer and fewer. So this is one area of concern, so you see increasing self-censorship. If you stop the independent-minded press upfront and advertisements are a crucial source of income, then this is the result that you get.

I think two things are very important. The first is that the commercial sector itself must realize what are the implications for them, for their own commercial activities, for their independence and their ability to make business decisions without political interference, if they take a short-term view that by giving in and capitulating to demands from Beijing, that that is the best way forward. It is not. Because my experience is that if you roll over and if you pull your punches, it does not encourage Beijing to take a more moderate line. They will just demand more the next time around.

So the business sector's awareness and the business sector's courage in speaking up and saying, "Hey, this will not do; if you do this, then we must re-think about whether Hong Kong remains an attractive place for us to invest in and to live and work in."

The other is, I think the media as a whole—I know that there are considerable pressures on media and increasing competition. It is entirely understandable that maybe they will tiptoe around sensitive subjects like human rights and whatnot, but again, the same argument goes.

So we need more coverage, we need more people prepared to talk about it, and above all we need more in the business sector who are prepared to stand up to this sort of arm twisting.

Representative MEADOWS. Well, thank you both for that. I want to follow up because I was hoping that you would touch on that. We've heard a number of different stories where this, as you would call it, the media doing their self-sanctioning, so to speak, but it really becomes an economic pressure and as an elected official I can assure you there's a number of media outlets I would love to sanction and make sure that they——

[Laughter].

Representative MEADOWS. However, that is not what makes us great, or our country great. So how do we best highlight this issue, because it is not happening just in Hong Kong, it's happening in a number of other countries within the region who do business with a number of Chinese companies. We're hearing more and more reports of either advertising that gets pulled or encouragement to not cover a particular area.

So this would not only go with human rights but with elections, with a number of other areas when you do not have, what I would say, a very inspective media. How do we put the pressure there without China seeing it as us interfering with their sovereignty, of which we would support as well? We understand that. So how do we best approach that, other than asking for somebody to be patriotic and take a punch in the nose?

Mr. LEE. Well, let's be realistic. What any foreign government does or says which offends Beijing will be condemned. You just cannot get out from that. If you believe that China ought to improve here or there and you say so, they avoid that. And the Chinese Government will say, ''mind your own business.''

But, I suggest that there is a good response to that, namely, Hong Kong is not China's internal affairs, because China has voluntarily made it an international affair by signing the international treaty with Great Britain over Hong Kong and having it registered with the United Nations.

Even more importantly, before the Sino-British Joint Declaration was first announced in public, the Chinese Government and the British government worked very hard to get the support of the international community, for it was feared that without international support, there would be massive emigration from Hong Kong. And they were immensely successful in their effort.

So when the Joint Declaration was first announced September 26, 1984, many governments came out openly and applauded it, including the U.S. Government, because these governments believed that the Joint Declaration would work, with the promise that all our core values specifically mentioned in it would be preserved for 50 years unchanged.

Thus your government has a good answer: ''Hong Kong is our business because you made it our business. You wanted us to support you. And we supported you; and we still support you. So please make it work.''

Of course, any businessman in the States wishing to invest in China would be very concerned if there is no free flow of economic information, true information, about a particular company that he wishes to invest in.

So if I were an American businessman investing in China, I would obviously support the freedom of the press in Hong Kong, to make sure that there is a free flow of economic information there. But the trouble is that, too many overseas business people prefer to take a short-term view, and adopt a cowardly and selfish stance, by leaving it to other people to speak up. For they don't want to jeopardize their business opportunities in China. But if they all cave in like this, their interest, they will all eventually suffer. I am also concerned that even foreign chambers of commerce are not speaking up. I can understand if individual members of these chambers do not have the guts to speak up, but that makes it more important that their chambers of commerce which represent them should speak up. But I have to say that very few—if any—speak up. This is our experience in Hong Kong.

Ms. CHAN. I think it's important for the United States' administration and for large organizations and governments everywhere to take an unequivocal and principled stance on their core values—of which press freedom is a very important core value—because whatever the initial reaction from Beijing, I think ultimately it invites more respect.

I was hearing from one of the reporters—I think it was Paul Mooney who was complaining about how he couldn't get a visa and whatnot. Well, my immediate reaction to that was, well, maybe two can play at the same game.

Representative MEADOWS. So your suggestion then would be a firmer response from the administration in terms of—instead of trying to say, well, gosh, highlight the problem and saying work with us, is a firmer response in terms of not only what we expect, but with regards to visas, I guess as you're pointing out, is to say that denial of visas here would have a retaliatory effect in the United States. Is that what you're suggesting?

Ms. CHAN. No. All I'm suggesting is that if you are concerned that journalists are not able to go about their legitimate business and their legitimate business is not just in the interests of this government and the people here, but also, I think, in the interests of China as a whole and the entire world, then the government should consider whether it is better to tiptoe around and hem and haw rather than take very principled steps.

Representative MEADOWS. All right.

Let me go a little bit further. So if we look at perhaps elections that are coming up, the independence of the judicial area, if we do not have the freedom of the press, how are we to rely in terms of those particular issues in terms of, are they truly independent, as they relate to Hong Kong? How do we make the best determinations here in the United States in terms of the narrative that is out there? Are there other forms of media, Facebook, Twitter? I mean, do those become the way to get the truth out there, or how do we do that?

Mr. LEE. It may well be so because they are more difficult to control. Hong Kong newspapers are so easy to control, and radio stations, and television stations, too. Recently, the Hong Kong Government made the Hong Kong people very angry when it changed its position drastically and unreasonably on the issue of licenses to free television stations. Originally the government announced that if an applicant can fulfill all the requirements, it will be given a license. It also said that there would be no limit as to the number of licenses. Three TV stations applied, and the government's own advisors found that all three were eligible. But the government decided that it would issue licenses only to two of them, which had been operating in Hong Kong for many years. But as one of those two is so hopeless that there has never been any competition between the existing two stations. But the third TV station, whose application was refused, would have brought genuine competition to the market. Although the government can control radio and television broadcasts, there is hope that, with the advancement of modern technology, Facebook, Twitter, and others, it will still be difficult for the government to control the freedom of expression, at least, in the near future.

Representative MEADOWS. Well, I have heard reports, and I'll let you follow up, that those Facebook, Twitter, whatever it may be, social media, goes along and as long as those issues are non-controversial, that they continue on with the free flow. The minute that they get more controversial in nature, that there is a number of initiatives that happen that don't allow the free flow of information. Is that what you experienced or heard?

Ms. CHAN. It is true that in the mainland there are attempts even to interfere and to censor social media, the Internet, and whatnot. Fortunately—and I hope for a long, long while—this is not yet the case in Hong Kong. Young people today largely communicate, and you would be surprised how quickly word spreads through social media, through mobile telephone text messages.

Representative MEADOWS. There are times when I'm not so surprised.

[Laughter].

Ms. CHAN. But in response to your question, I think that if the media practices self-censorship and the truth is not getting out, it's so much more important that the movers and shakers in this country and elsewhere come to Hong Kong to visit and see for themselves what is actually happening on the ground.

We need more professionals, people in the legal profession, people, journalists, to come and see the state of health of the press, the state of health of our legal profession, and the state of health of the rule of law. All these will give you a much more accurate picture instead of simply relying on the sense of the press and on routine reports that are turned up.

Mr. LEE. On the rule-of-law front, there are worrying signs. First, about two years ago, Mr. Xi Jinping, now the President of China came to Hong Kong in the capacity of Vice President, said to the Chief Justice of Hong Kong on a public occasion and in the presence of all senior government officials, that judges must cooperate with the government. That shows he has little regard for the separation of powers.

Then, on the occasion of the retirement of a senior judge of the Court of Final Appeal, he said openly that "a storm of unprecedented ferocity is approaching." He was referring to the rule of law. So the rule of law is clearly under threat.

Representative MEADOWS. Well, I'm going to close on mine because we've got very capable staff here that are very prepared and much more able to ask the piercing questions that perhaps will illuminate some of the issues.

But I want to close with this last question. How do we best address these issues, whether they be human rights issues, trade issues, freedom of the press issues, without the Chinese people believing that it is antagonistic toward them? Because that is not the intent of most Americans.

Most Americans see it as a relationship; that they want to have a good relationship based on mutual trust and respect, but yet when you identify these areas it can sometimes appear to be more antagonistic. How do we best identify the problems, address them without the antagonistic rhetoric or meaning behind it for the Chinese people?

Mr. LEE. I would not pretend to be able to give any advice to you, Congressman, or your very able staff. But I would have thought, as always, that we should call a spade a spade.

I've just had a quick glance at a few pages of your report on Hong Kong. It was beautifully done. You told the truth about Hong Kong. You do not antagonize anybody, and you tell the truth plainly.

Ms. CHAN. Can I add, I think trust is a two-way street. There has to be a willingness to compromise, to accommodate each other's differences, and perhaps even sometimes to agree to disagree. I think we need to point out that we have an international treaty. Hong Kong is an international city.

I spent my entire career in the public service and I remember, both in the immediate run-up to 1997 and in the years following, certainly in the four years that I still served with the SAR [Special Administrative Region] Government, we were regularly rolled out to come to this country, to other countries, to instill confidence in the Joint Declaration and the Basic Law, to say you have nothing to worry about, it will be business as usual, there will be "one country, two systems," and the rights and freedoms that Hong Kong people enjoy and the rule of law will remain intact.

Nothing has changed since then. What we are asking is an entirely doable deal. We're asking no more than that Beijing honors its promise to the people of Hong Kong. That is good not just for us, but for China as a whole and for the rest of the world.

I am Chinese. Martin is Chinese. We regard ourselves every bit a patriot. But in my definition, being a patriot does not mean I have to agree with everything that the Central Government is doing, nor do I necessarily have to preach the Communist cause. This is the whole difference between one country and two systems.

I want to see a strong China, but I believe a strong China cannot be just strong in economic terms, but has to be strong in terms of the leadership's confidence in the way it deals with its own people and its respect for human dignity and in giving to its people basic rights and freedoms.

Now, Hong Kong has always been a model in this respect and all we ask is that you allow us to continue to keep our identity, because we believe that—in that way—we are best able to serve our country not only in sustainable long-term economic growth in the mainland, but also in assisting our country to become a truly international player.

Representative MEADOWS. Well said. Thank you both for your illuminating testimony. I am going to turn it over to our very capable staff. I apologize for monopolizing the time.

Ms. CHAN. Thank you very much.

Mr. LEE. Thank you.

Mr. PROTIC. Ms. Chan and Mr. Lee, thank you again for coming to testify at the roundtable. Thank you for your courage, your patriotism. We appreciate it.

Ms. CHAN. Thank you.

Mr. PROTIC. The Basic Law requires a candidate for chief executive to be nominated by a broadly representative nominating committee. Have you seen any indication from either the central government or the Hong Kong Government about exactly how broadly representative the nominating committee for the 2017 chief executive election will be?

Ms. CHAN. Well, we take the Basic Law as it stands. The Basic Law says that the nominating committee for the nomination and election of the Chief Executive shall be broadly representative and that the nomination process shall be a democratic process. We are currently engaged in arguing exactly what do these words mean.

In the eyes of the Hong Kong people, it is pretty straightforward. There can be no arguments about what is meant by ''broadly representative'' and ''democratic process.'' Yet, we hear time and again from Beijing officials, coming to Hong Kong, and from the pro-Beijing forces in Hong Kong that it means totally different things. There is a serious attempt afoot to rewrite the provisions in the Basic Law as to how you constitute the nominating committee.

In short, what we are saying is to meet the criteria laid down in the Basic Law. We want a set of universal suffrage proposals that gives choice to the voters, that does not attempt to set down unreasonable restrictions to stop anybody from standing for election as a Chief Executive and third, that you cannot reject anybody who happens to have different political affiliations from the ones that Beijing may prefer.

On this basis, I think at the end of the day we will look to see what sort of credible proposals this government comes up with; in the meantime I have to stress Beijing seems to want to force down our throat a set of proposals essentially which will ensure a rigged election and will guarantee them 100 percent that their anointed candidate will win. That is not what we are seeking.

Mr. PROTIC. Thank you.

Mr. LIU. Our staff has one more question and I'll turn it over to David Petrick to ask a question. Thanks.

Mr. PETRICK. Thanks for coming.

I was wondering if you could speak to the political environment within Hong Kong, specifically what the attitude of the current Hong Kong Government is toward implementing universal suffrage.

Ms. CHAN. We unfortunately have a Chief Executive who has now been in post for two years, but who has not convinced the community that he either shares our core values or is committed to implementing ''one country, two systems.'' He has not taken a leading role in forging a consensus on universal suffrage. He has relegated this task to his Chief Secretary, Mrs. Carrie Lam, and she is doing a very difficult job in a very difficult situation.

The feeling of the community overwhelmingly is that CY, the Chief Executive, is not going to stick his neck out, is not going to speak on behalf of the Hong Kong people, but will take instructions from Beijing. So it underlines the urgency for Hong Kong people to use this period, before the government comes up with concrete proposals, to lay out exactly what the minimum acceptable deal is since we cannot, unfortunately, rely on the SAR Government to take the lead.

It is a great pity because we know that, given the sharp divide in public opinion on how to move forward on universal suffrage, and bearing in mind we need to secure two-thirds majority in our legislature and we need to secure the approval of the central government, it is crucially important that the government be willing to take a leadership role in this whole discussion. But we are so far not seeing that.

Mr. LEE. May I elaborate a little? This Government of Hong Kong doesn't decide on this important question. It's waiting for instructions from Beijing, period.

Mr. LIU. Okay. Thank you.

Just real quickly, we have a few more minutes left. I know we started a little bit late. I wanted to give the audience a chance to ask a question or two, if we could try to fit that in. I would just ask you to keep your question brief. We have some mics in the room so if you have a question, if you want to go back to—sure. Sure.

Ms. WORDEN. Hello, I'm Minky Worden from Human Rights Watch. You paint a rather distressing picture of the current environment in Hong Kong. But can you tell us about the younger people, those who perhaps were only born at the time of the handover? What is their attitude, what is their approach? Are they prepared to defend the freedoms and the rule of law in Hong Kong that they have grown up with?

Mr. LEE. Well, I can think of two good reasons why there is hope. The first, is sitting to my left, Anson Chan.

[Laughter].

Mr. LEE. Now, for many years she was in government. She was the most senior person in government next to the Chief Executive, both before and after the handover of sovereignty to China. In those days I used to argue with her, though not on everything. But now she's on my side. She has been making stronger arguments than I've done today. You can see that.

The other reason is a young guy of 17 years of age called Joshua Wong. He's still in secondary school. About one-and-a-half years ago it was suddenly revealed that the Hong Kong Government was trying to brainwash our kids. He spearheaded a movement which started with about 20 students demonstrating in the streets, and nobody paid any attention to it.

Later on, some parents joined together because they didn't want their kids to be brainwashed. But again, only 100, 200 people demonstrated. But within a short time, a hundred thousand people demonstrated outside the government headquarters. And that caused the government to withdraw its plan of brainwashing our children. Can you imagine a young student of 16 at the time leading such a big movement? So these are two good reasons, Anson Chan and Joshua Wong, why there is hope in Hong Kong.

Ms. CHAN. I think the real hope lies with the people of Hong Kong, a majority of whom treasure our values and are prepared to stand up and be counted.

Mr. LIU. Okay. We have time for one more question. You, sir?

Mr. ZEITLIN. My name is Arnold Zeitlin and I had various associations with Hong Kong over the past 20 years. For Martin, I'd like to ask when the Democrats will get their act together, and for Ms. Chan, I would like to ask what your reaction has been to the reaction to your proposal to reshape, or shape, the nominating committee.

Mr. LEE. Well, the Democrats always get their act together when they're under great pressure. And they are under great pressure now. So I expect them to get their act together pretty soon.

Ms. CHAN. Well, the initial reaction to our proposal which we have put forward a month ago has been better than I expected. What we did was, given the sharp divide in public opinion, we tried to find a course of action that conforms with what the government wished to see, which is to bring everything back, all proposals back within the strict parameter of the Basic Law. This is what we did.

But at the same time we addressed the fundamental problem, which is, how do you make the nominating committee broadly representative? How do you prevent Beijing having a say right from the start, from the nominating process to the standing for elections? Of course, finally, they have the ultimate authority to appoint or not appoint the Chief Executive.

So we have broadened the nominating committee from 1,200 to 1,400 and widened the franchise to all 3.4 million registered voters in Hong Kong who will have a right to participate in nominating a chief executive. And for anybody who wants to stand for Chief Executive, all he needs to do, or she needs to do, is to secure 140 nominations from this 1,400-strong nominating committee to get in.

Mr. ZEITLIN. Does it have a chance?

Ms. CHAN. I would like to think it has a chance. The important thing is to try—when we get back, we will have more discussions within the community, particularly within the pan-democratic camp and I'm hoping that somehow the pan-democratic camp will be able to come up with a set of proposals which we can unite behind, because then I think we stand a better chance of securing agreement.

Mr. LIU. Okay. Thank you.

I wanted to close the roundtable here. We have run out of time. I wanted to enter our Cochairman Congressman Chris Smith's statement into the record.

I thank the audience for coming and most of all thank you, Ms. Chan and Mr. Lee, for helping us understand better here in Washington, in the United States, a very important issue that has not been getting enough attention, but I think that you have helped at least start a conversation here about that. So thank you again for coming, and this roundtable is adjourned.

Ms. CHAN. We thank you for this opportunity.

[Applause].

[The prepared statement of Representative Christopher Smith appears in the appendix.]

[Whereupon, at 1:11 p.m. the roundtable was concluded.]

A P P E N D I X

PREPARED STATEMENTS

PREPARED STATEMENT OF HON. SHERROD BROWN, A U.S. SENATOR FROM OHIO; CHAIRMAN, CONGRESSIONAL-EXECUTIVE COMMISSION ON CHINA

APRIL 3, 2014

Anson Chan and Martin Lee are here at a critical time for Hong Kong. The future of freedom and democracy in Hong Kong is under serious threat.

China promised to let the people of Hong Kong freely elect their leaders and enjoy the freedoms of speech, press, and religion.

China is backtracking on these promises.

In just three short years, the people of Hong Kong are to elect their leader, the Chief Executive, in the first election by "universal suffrage." But we know that China is already placing "pre-conditions" on who can run, raising serious doubts about whether the elections will be free and fair.

The environment for press freedom in Hong Kong is deteriorating. Incidents of violence and harassment against journalists have risen. Hong Kong's media faces ever-increasing pressure from mainland China.

This Commission has made it a priority to monitor and report on developments in Hong Kong, and we will continue to do so.

We, in Congress and on this Commission, must hold China accountable for its commitments. We must continue to listen and learn from people like our distinguished panelists today.

Too much is at stake for Hong Kong, mainland China, and the international community.

At the end of the day, Hong Kong is not just a financial center of 7 million people.

It is a test of China's commitment to the internationally recognized rights of people everywhere to freely elect their leaders and to enjoy basic freedoms.

It is a test of whether China will allow genuine democracy and freedom to take root in Hong Kong.

I urge China to follow through on its commitments.

PREPARED STATEMENT OF HON. CHRISTOPHER SMITH, A U.S. REPRESENTATIVE FROM NEW JERSEY; COCHAIRMAN, CONGRESSIONAL-EXECUTIVE COMMISSION ON CHINA

APRIL 3, 2014

Today's roundtable examines the prospects for democracy and press freedom in Hong Kong. Thanks to our two guests, Martin Lee and Anson Chan, for joining us here today, and for their years of dedication to working for freedom and democracy in Hong Kong. We look forward to hearing their thoughts on the future of Hong Kong.

Under the "one country, two systems" model, China guaranteed that Hong Kong could retain its separate political, legal, and economic systems for at least 50 years. Hong Kong's constitution, the Basic Law, protects the rights of the people of Hong Kong to free speech, assembly, and the power to choose their own government, ultimately through universal suffrage.

This is clearly what is wanted by the people of Hong Kong, but increasingly, it seems, Beijing is unprepared to allow the people of Hong Kong to select leaders of their own choosing.

Although China's central government agreed that universal suffrage would be implemented in time for the 2017 Chief Executive elections, recent statements by Chinese officials raise concerns that results will be fixed permanent in Beijing's favor.

In Beijing, Qiao Xiaoyang, head of the Law Committee of the National People's Congress Standing Committee, demanded not only that candidates for Chief Executive must "love the country and love Hong Kong," but also that they must "not confront the central government."

In Hong Kong, Secretary for Justice Rimsky Yuen stated that the International Covenant on Civil and Political Rights does not apply to Hong Kong's elections, despite the fact that Article 39 of Hong Kong's Basic Law clearly states that the ICCPR would remain in force in Hong Kong after the 1997 handover.

Beijing's attempt to stack the deck against democracy is disappointing, but not surprising to those who have watched China continually backpedal on its promises to the people of Hong Kong.

The freedoms of the people of Hong Kong to choose their own government, to vote freely, and to stand for election are being called into question when there should be no question.

Hong Kong's continued autonomy and the advance of its democracy is a concern of the U.S. Congress and of freedom-loving peoples everywhere.

We are also concerned about the steady erosion of press freedoms in Hong Kong. According to the Press Index published by Reporters Without Borders, over the past decade Hong Kong's ranking has dropped from 34th to 61st.

Two recent attacks have drawn attention to the deteriorating state of freedom of the press. In February of this year, Kevin Lau, recently dismissed as editor of the Ming Pao newspaper, was severely injured in a knife attack in broad day light. Less than a month later, two employees of the Hong Kong Morning News were beaten with metal pipes by masked men.

Earlier this year, after outspoken radio host Li Wei-ling was fired, she publicly blamed the Chief Executive and the government of Hong Kong for pressuring her radio station in order to ''[suppress] . . . freedom of the press.''

This trend is a chilling reminder that Beijing seeks to control both the media and the political process in Hong Kong. These actions raise critical questions whether the ''one country, two systems'' model can ever fully guarantee human rights and democracy for the people of Hong Kong.

If given a real choice, people everywhere vote to advance representative governments that protect the rule of law and the fundamental freedoms of speech, assembly, association, and religion. The people of Mainland China do not have such a choice and attempts to pursue universally-recognized rights are often met with brutality and harassment.

This cannot be Hong Kong's future.

Hong Kong is the true embodiment of the ''China Dream'' and that fact may scare some in the Communist Party. We stand with those who want Hong Kong to remain free, vital, prosperous, and democratic—as Beijing has long promised.

ABOUT THE AUTHOR

The Congressional-Executive Commission on China was created by Congress in October 2000 with the legislative mandate to monitor human rights and the development of the rule of law in China, and to submit an annual report to the President and the Congress. The Commission consists of nine Senators, nine Members of the House of Representatives, and five senior Administration officials appointed by the President.